Launcelot Cranmer-Byng

Poems of Paganism

Songs of Life and Love

Launcelot Cranmer-Byng

Poems of Paganism
Songs of Life and Love

ISBN/EAN: 9783337408572

Printed in Europe, USA, Canada, Australia, Japan

Cover: Foto ©Thomas Meinert / pixelio.de

More available books at **www.hansebooks.com**

POEMS OF PAGANISM;

OR,

SONGS OF LIFE AND LOVE.

BY

"PAGANUS"

(L. CRANMER-BYNG.)

LONDON:

THE ROXBURGHE PRESS,

3, *Victoria Street*,
Westminster,
and
32, *Charing Cross, S.W.*

MDCCCXCV.

DEDICATION.

GEORGE BARLOW.

Phoebus! wherever thou lightest, joy fol-
lows;
Heart of man wakens to music, and
sings :—
" Glad are the rays that are Phoebus Apollo's,
Golden the hours of delight that he
brings."

Strong-hearted, lyre-loving God of the morning,
Darkness and falsehood shall shudder and
flee,
Gloom-mantled crime at thy presence take
warning,
Earth wake from sleep at the vision of
thee.

God of the truth that shines clear in the day-
time,
Light of the soul that hath wandered in
night,
Phoebus, oh, hearken, thou God of love's May-
time,
Lord of love's seasonless summer delight !

Who is it comes with the sunlight above
him,
Holding the sun-smitten lyre in his hand,
Making the hearts of us listen and love
him,
Sending a thrill through the night-weary
land ?

Who is it lightens the load of our yearning,
Shows us the sun of our darkened desire ?
Music so passionate, beautiful, burning,
Surely no mortal could wake from the
lyre !

"This is my servant. The lyre of my
giving
Trembles to tell the sad spirits that
sleep

Night-dreams are over now Phoebus is
 living,
See! the doomed darkness dies over the
 deep."

God-gifted singer of truth and of passion—
 Truth that is dawning, and love that is
 free—
Fain were my poor little numbers to fashion
 Song that should hallow both Phoebus and
 thee.

Lacking the lyre, with the pipe that was
 hidden
 Deep in the soil by some shepherd of yore,
Made I the songs that I send thee unbidden.
 Let them not trouble thee. Where the
 streets roar;

Where the loud market with thousands is
 thronging;
 Where the gold Moloch rears proudly his
 head;
These will be silent, nor fill thee with longing
 For the green meads, and the days that
 are dead.

Only for song-time and summer these numbers,
  Where trees are many and mortals are
    few ;
Where in the forest Pan wakens from slumbers.
  Take them. I leave them to Nature and
    you.

CONTENTS.

9

A PATRIOT POET

O THE heart of England yearns
For a melody that burns,
For a young god from Olympus—all the
  morning's flush desire
In the chords that throb and quiver
As the sunlight on the river
From the hand that stirs to music all the
  harp's imprisoned fire.

To a nation overwrought
In the wilderness of thought
O'er your pessimistic babble, little middlemen
  of rhyme,
Down the years that damn and dull us
Pants the passion of Catullus,
Calls the seraph-soul of Shelley—Byron's
  rebel-heart sublime.

You may persecute the brave,
Ply your scourge upon the slave,
But the blood of all the martyrs only swells
    the tide of truth,
As it rolls serenely forward
To the billows beating shoreward,
And the sea and river mingle in the fiery lips
    of youth.

God has written on your walls,
And the voice of freedom falls
On the ears of weary Titans, as they dream
    upon the soil.
And the world shall pause in wonder
As they rend their bonds asunder,
As the lyre's triumphant thunder sounds the
    knell of sunless toil.

A PRAYER FOR PEACE

To the God of hapless beauty, to the Lord of
    saddest song,
To the Guardian of that garden where all
    broken hearts belong,—
Of the poppy-sprinkled garden, where for ever
    sets the sun,
Where lost lovers meet and mingle all their
    spirit-life in one,
Where red passion strays—a phantom of the
    flame that flared and sped,
Where the dreamer lies a-dreaming of the
    rapture that is dead,—
Hear me, Lord, and dragon-watch o'er the
    souls that peaceful dream,
With the walls of brass around them and the
    ever-circling stream ;
For my heart is torn and bleeding, and the
    soul of me is fain
For a cycle of the slumber that should ease
    me of my pain.

I have battled, I was beaten, and my captive
    heart lies bound
By the sorrows that beset me, by the griefs
    that gathered round.
I have sought the old-world shadows for their
    silence that would keep,
For their sepulchres to save me from the
    tossing, moaning deep :
But a voice cried : " On for ever !   Thou shalt
    never know the shore,
Nor thy battered galley shelter from the
    storms that are in store."
So I steered in desperation for the far-off
    western waves,
For the garden of my vision, where love's
    phantoms find their graves,
And the chill winds of religion howled around
    my lonely soul,
And the mocking voice cried : "Onward !
    Thou shalt never find the goal."
But I came to thee, great Guardian of the
    broken hearts that lay
Where the noontide sun of passion fades to
    crimson streams away,
Where two hearts are bound together in the
    poppy-purpled sleep,

And their sepulchres have saved them from
the tossing, moaning deep.
O thou guardian of the garden where lost
lovers lie and dream,
With the walls of brass around them and the
ever-circling stream,
Shall I never, never enter? Shall my spirit
never rest
In the garden that lies dreaming in the
splendour of the West?

ALL THAT I HAVE.

I CANNOT veil the past
Whose gloomy shadows cast
Their awful length of blackness on your life ;
    But take this hand to guide
    And steer you down the tide,
This loving breast to shield you through the
    strife.

    All that I have is yours—
    A passion that endures,
A heart to follow music unto truth,
    A soul that cannot quail
    From very shame to fail,
And all the deep devotedness of youth.

    Faith is not mine to give :
    Enough for me I live
To aid some fellow-being to the sun,
    Whose mild and mellow rays
    Shall light those happy days
When all our hopeless seeking shall be done.

I may not faultless be,
Sin stains my purity,
And sorrow in my heart holds bitter feast ;
But love has power to save
From dark dishonour's grave
A soul that never herded with the beast.

Ah ! give me of that love,
That I may worthy prove,
And, hand in hand, redemption we will seek,
Through life's vast loneliness,
Through trouble and distress,
Till time has kissed the teardrops from your
cheek.

AU REVOIR—NOT ADIEU!

AU REVOIR—not Adieu ! For the thought
of our parting
Strikes chill on the heart that beats only
for you ;
Ere soul forsakes soul, into solitude starting,
By all that was love, Au Revoir—not
Adieu !

Au Revoir—not Adieu. As I clasp you and
kiss you—
More true than a mistress, more tender
than wife—
My heart cannot learn its sad lesson to miss
you,
To tear out the tendrils of love from my
life.

18

Au Revoir—not Adieu! Like a knell that is
    tolling,
The bell for departure rings agony dumb;
And lips madly meet for some sweetness
    consoling,
    Some wish to conceal that the parting has
    come.

Little girl, with your brown eyes of innocent
    wonder,
    Little rosebud so ruthlessly brought into
    bloom,
The sword of adversity sweeps us asunder;
    But love, like a beacon, shall glow through
    the gloom.

Au Revoir—not Adieu! For a time we must
    sever;
    But the grass has its green, and the sea has
    its blue,
And you have my heart—keep it, darling, for
    ever:
    Fate parts, love abides. Au Revoir—not
    Adieu!

CHRISTIAN AND PAGAN.

Christian.

TENDER and true she waits for you
  In the beautiful burnished skies ;
Your darling waits at the jewelled gates
  Of the garden of Paradise.

Pagan.

Alas ! my friend, and is this the end
  Of a love that lived like ours :
To view one's own on a golden throne,
  With a diadem of flowers ;

To hear her play on a harp alway ;
  See nightgown frippery fold
About her waist ? Has Heaven no taste
  For a woman of lovely mould ?

And the songs I taught—will they count for
  aught,
Those wonderful heathen lays ?
No, no ! She'll hymn for an angel's whim,
  Through the tedious golden days.

Each fond embrace is a dire disgrace,
  With the eye of God above,
And the saints would blush, as His voice said :
  " Hush !
Ye must put away your love."

Calm, cold, and pure, ye may endure ;
  Yet passion shall pine with drouth
For love's fair form, and the kisses warm
  Of her beautiful burning mouth.

No Heaven for me, but the dancing sea,
  And the far-off Lydian shore ;
Where, hand in hand, in her own bright land,
  We'll linger and love once more.

And she shall sing to the lute I bring,
  And sorrow and care and pain.
Shall pass away with the dying day,
  And night shall return again.

Then with the night comes lost delight :
Love lurks in each dreamy dale,
Whose eyes shall be the starry sea,
And whose voice the nightingale.

CLOUD, WIND, AND RAIN.

A MIST came out of the sea,
And a cloud fell over my heart:
But the mist and the cloud were part
Of a shadow that haunted me.

A moan went over the wave,
And cold on my spirit fell
The doom of a tolling bell,
And the thud of a closing grave.

Then rain swept under the skies,
And tears coursed over my cheek,
For the love that I vainly seek,
And the light of her dear lost eyes.

But night fled into the west,
And hope dawned out of my fears.
Love smiled upon sunlit tears,
And sorrow was fain to rest.

CONCERNING TRUTH AND ART.

THOUGH perchance no mortal numbers have
the power to wake from slumbers
All the silent spirits sleeping in the darkness and the mist,
Still I'll sing the veiled stars gleaming, far
beyond your hopeless dreaming,
Who have followed marsh-lights streaming
to the doom ye daren't resist.

If I cannot climb the mountains, let me seek
secluded fountains,
Where the naiads lurk and listen to the
waters as they fall,
Weaving webs of fancy round me, where the
old-world magic found me,
Where love's flowery fetters bound me, too
ethereal to pall.

Though ye drive me to perdition in the zeal
  of superstition,
'Tis your Master that ye martyr in each
  sacerdotal soul.
From your Golgothas descending, follow not
  with spite unending
Hearts their sunward journey wending,
  thoughts no poet can control.

'Tis some awful power that plays us on this
  mournful stage ; arrays us,
Some in rags and some in purple, for the
  parts we fill untried,
To a scene for ever shifting, to a curtain ever
  lifting,
On our flotsam spirits drifting into darkness
  deified.

God made singer to discover, with the keen
  eye of a lover,
All the cherished hidden secrets only
  Nature's darlings know ;
What bright rapture burns and blushes by
  the gurgling tide that gushes
Down deep inlets among rushes when the
  springtime blossoms blow.

Art is sweet, but never, maiden, where the
    dells with dreams are laden;
  Darkness loves red roses better than the
    day loves roses white;
All the sense of sweetly sinning, life's old
    drama new beginning,
  Love triumphant, passion winning, wait the
    dark wings of the night.

Drooping heart, let all disown thee; let each
    passing bigot stone thee;
  Let their demon malice dog thee through
    the ever-circling shade.
Music's star shines fair above thee; loyal souls
    shall learn to love thee;
  Persecution only prove thee fearless soldier
    undismayed.

Yes! if one sad soul might hear me, if my
    music might endear me
  To some lonely hero, fighting, grandly
    conscious of his doom!
He shall clasp my hand for ever, though vast
    leagues of ocean sever,
  Though these mortal eyes may never see
    the sunrise gild the gloom.

CUPID'S SLEEP.

SMOTHERED in roses, drenched in dew,
Sleep-flushed eyelids heavily pressed,
Half revealed, half hidden from view,
Cupid lies on the earth's green breast,
With a gush of notes from a thousand throats
For a lullaby, breathed o'er his dainty nest.

Hour by hour, in the dim moonlight,
Arrows had flashed from his deadly bow ;
And now he slumbers and dreams of night,
Red Eve and her passionate after-glow,
Of all the grace of a tell-tale face,
And the warm, wild words that are whispered
      low.

DESPAIR.

SHE has left me the weight of a secret unspoken—
A love half revealed in her sorrow-kissed
 eyes.
Down the night of despair goes a heart that is
 broken
 To the hell of lost hope, where the worm
 never dies.

She has sped from the sphere of my being for
 ever ;
 She has left but a trail on the cloud-ridden
 track ;
But if pride had not parted, no shadow could
 sever,
 And the heart she has trampled would
 welcome her back.

Though I stretch out vain hands to a form
  that evades me,
And pine for a voice that is utterly still,
Yet only in dreams her dear image upbraids
  me,
And the hand of remorse on my bosom
  falls chill.

Can the power that united us cleave us
  asunder—
The forces that lured us, so suddenly part ?
'Tis the soul answers " No " on the echoing
  thunder ;
But the moan of despair sweeps a desolate
  heart.

GOOD-BYE, LOVE!

SINCE I cannot compel you to love me
　I will take to the forest my pain,
Where the green leaves of summer above me
　Will banish the thought of disdain.

I will pour out my musical sorrow
　To nature, than beauty more kind,
And my lute shall from Æolus borrow
　The lilt of his wandering wind.

If I cannot compel you to render
　The love I had died to possess,
I shall still find the nightingale tender,
　Still welcome the moonbeam's caress.

In my heart just a shadow of sadness,
　On my lips just the ghost of a sigh,
With a tear for the tremors of madness,
　Sweet star of love's morning, good-bye!

On my lips just the ghost of a sigh, love,
  In my heart just a shadow of pain,
With a tear for our parting,—good-bye, love !
  Good-bye, little soul of disdain!

HAUNTED.

There's a burden I cannot banish
  In the long, lone hours of grief;
It recedes, but will never vanish;
  It saddens, but brings relief;

It sighs o'er the sunken ashes
  Of days that are past recall,
And loud the wind it lashes
  Round fancy's funeral hall.

As I follow, entranced, and listen,
  The meaning I half divine
Of the dews that in dark eyes glisten,
  And spangle the night in mine.

Ah! they tell of love's billows breaking
  The barriers man has set,
Of passion from dream awaking,
  Wild yearning, and vain regret.

And I still hear the music rolling,
  And shudder between the bars,
Though her knell they have long ceased
    tolling,
  And her soul's beyond the stars.

HEART OF STONE.

IN my heart a tune is ringing
That some strolling bard was singing
　　When the chill of parting came,
　　Breathing a beloved name ;
　　And the blinding tears fell fast
　　For the passion of the past.

Down the stricken night it waileth,
Till the demon darkness paleth,
　　And the weary watcher slips
　　Into dream with parted lips—
　　Pallid face of wan despair,
　　And the moonbeams in his hair.

Mournful numbers, madness bringing,
In my breast your burden flinging,
　　Tell me, shall I never see
　　One whose love is life to me ?
　　Heart of grief, be heart of stone !
　　You must bear the cross alone.

HESITATION.

SHALL I pause on the brink for a moment to
 shiver,
To peer into gloom that is dark as the grave ?
Or, scornful of self, launch my barque on the
 river,
Cast care to the current, and trust to the wave ?
O thou God, of this shuddering spirit the giver;
What light for the lonely, what hope for the
 slave ?

I made me a palace of wonder and pleasure,
 A garden of flowers in a land of delight ;
Each fount overflowed with song's infinite
 measure ;
 Mirth mellowed the day ; love enchanted
 the night :
All that passion could give of her tenderest
 treasure
 Was mine till the stars in their season took
 flight.

But frail are love's walls, and his palace must
    crumble,
  His garden grow weeds, and each fountain
    fall dumb ;
Man's babels of bliss are predestined to tumble,
  And the depths of remorse are there any
    can plumb ?
The tempest sweeps light o'er the lowly and
    humble,
  But the passionate heart in its pride must
    succumb.

The light of my soul—is it honour or glory ?
  The star of my song—is it wealth or
    renown ?
What way leads to truth not encrimsoned
    and gory ?
  What guerdon of valour, save martyrdom's
    crown ?
All ends are the same in life's pitiful story :
  The peerless and brave in the battle go
    down.

GOOD-BYE! good-bye to the hopes that were
    reared and shattered :
A last farewell to the hours whose life was
    flame.
Time never restores the blossoms his breath
    has scattered :
The stars still gleam, but their beauty is
    not the same.

The anchor's up, and our ship goes sweeping
    seaward ;
Her white keel severs the shuddering, wine-
    dark ways ;
But the billows of banished bliss come rolling
    me-ward,
And bear me back to the haven of happier
    days.

The past lies fair, with its vistas of light behind
  me
  Like some brief shadow of dream from a
    poppy-land ;
But bloomless garlands of sunless hope now
    bind me,
  And memory leaves but the touch of a
    darling hand.

In my far-off, sea-caressed home fond hearts
    are pleading :
  There are crowns to weave, there are visions
    of sunlit skies ;
But the fairest dream is ever the dream re-
    ceding,
  And the sweetest love is ever the love that
    flies.

IGNORANT ROSES.

BLUE Plymouth waters woo my sweet,
   Green Devon woodlands love her,
Red poppies meet her pretty feet,
   Brown branches wave above her.

Gold sunbeams, shattered in her hair,
   But glorify gold tresses,
And roses swear she is so fair
   They pine for her caresses.

Ah ! roses red, how can ye know
   The rapture of my lady ?
For love lies low where zephyrs blow
   In dream-dells cool and shady.

What wist ye of the nodding night,
   The thrill of moonlit kisses,
When, out of sight, love's warm delight
   Mates all your modest misses ?

LOUIS KOSSUTH.

WHO will mourn the undying dead
Gone into darkness, garlanded,
Fame's tender trophies around his head?

Who will mourn for a nation's night;
Weep for the woes of trampled right,
Sunless sorrow, and starless might?

Stained, bedewed with the blood of strife,
Freedom flashed on the hero life;
Lured his spirit when storms were rife.

Time unites what the sword may sever
Death may come, but oblivion never:
Louis Kossuth lives on for ever.

LIFE.

OH, earth and sky, I live! for love compelling
  Has filled the thirsty inlets of my soul.
I feel the fount of song within me welling,
  And passion's frenzied billows slip control.

For one fair woman's eyes, divinely tender,
  Mirrored in mine, have blinded them with
    love ;
Then rose my sun, my angel, my defender,
  Where calumny with lonely weakness
    strove.

I, who caressed the withered wanton Anguish,
  Supped off a sigh, and drained no toast but
    tears,
Doomed in the dungeons of despair to
    languish,
  Counting each hour a myriad mournful
    years—

I, whom the Levite left with pious loathing,
  Wounded and well-nigh perished from the
    drouth,
Waken to life, whom love, with pity clothing,
  Heals with the countless kisses of her
    mouth.

LIFT THE LYRE.

LIFT the lyre from failing fingers
  Ere the hand is cold and set ;
Still the fire of music lingers
  Where the strings with tears are wet.

You who loved him—softly taking,
  Place it on his peaceful breast ;
Nevermore the silence breaking
  Lord and lyre shall take their rest.

Do not mourn the dead musician ;
  Stay the tears ye idly shed.
Deep in poppy-bloom Elysian
  Let him lay his weary head.

Only weep for words unspoken,
  Sigh but for the songs unsung.
Death salutes him by this token—
  Whom the Gods love perish young.

LINUS TO LYTERSES.

WHAT of the past, Lyterses?
　What of the gathered years?
Time, with his tender mercies,
　Leaves not a stain of tears.

Where are the joys that bound us?
　Where are the songs we sung?
Where the warm hands that crowned us
　Kings, when the world was young?

Weary of life immortal
　Linus in languor nods,
Dreaming of death's dream-portal,
　Panting to sleep with gods.

Go, little gush of verses,
　Over Time's barren bars :
Whisper to lone Lyterses,—
　" Linus still seeks the stars."

LINKED TO THE PAST.

OUR roots strike deep into the soil of time,
The loam of perished ages holds us fast,
And though with heavenward glance we soar
    sublime,
We cannot wholly rid us of the past.
Still superstition croons, though Faith be
    gone,
And timid Conscience mumbles sadly on.

For dim ancestral spectres dog our ways,
Live in each varied mood, each passing
    thought.
From the drear store-house of their garnered
    days
Faint hopes, forgotten fears, old joys, en-
    wrought
Into the living brain, can often teach
A grander lesson than the parsons preach.

We wear the robes of dead humanity;
The cerements of our Fathers wrap us round ;
We cannot 'scape them, though we vainly try.
Dull matter weighs upon us : we are bound
By links of ancient virtue, former sin,
And perished deeds pursue their course within.

The fool abhors his earthly tenement,
And pines for hell in hopes of future bliss,
Raising of blood and tears a monument—
A lasting token—lest Jehovah miss
His glut of Christian gore. Why shun the
        sod,
Poor fool, when soul and matter meet in
        God ?

LOST IDEALS.

YOUTH fades, but the star that we loved and
  vowed to follow
And seek till the long night sank upon
  darkened eyes—
Has this, too, left us alone in the hateful
  hollow
  Where mute despair on the bosom of madness lies ?

Is there no faith in the far-off light that made
  us
  The hero souls that we seemed when the
  years were young ?
Will no dim gleam of our glorious trust up-
  braid us ?
  No memory rise and rebuke till the heart
  is wrung ?

47

One star soon fails ; but the lesson its beauty
    taught us,
  Shall this, too, fail when the current of life
    runs slack ;
When tyrannous Time and his henchman,
    Care, have sought us,
  And doubt's wan face ever peers o'er the
    waters black ?

The tiller slips from the stiffened hand that
    guided
  Hope's buoyant barque in her course
    through the moonless sea,
And the shuddering coward steers into port
    who prided
  His soul in its scorn of the waves, in the
    will of the free.

Still, far away, down the dark-browed night
    is streaming
  Truth's burning star in its glory and
    grandeur lone ;
It kindles the young, it colours e'en childhood's
    dreaming,
  But old men sleep, and forget that it ever
    shone.

LOVE AND THE LARK.

O YOU so fair, whose glorious hair,
  Bright aureole, beams above you,
Your beauty fires a thousand lyres
  Whose masters madly love you.

O you so sweet, whose tiny feet
  Made glad the gloom around me,
Though none came near the darkness drear
  Where true love sought and found me,

Your lips redeemed the heart that dreamed,
  With love's own tender token ;
Then passion came, with eyes aflame,
  And all sweet words unspoken

Shaped into song, and fled along
  In numbers wildly splendid,
Flashed through the dark, and told the lark
  How nobly night was ended.

" Awake ! awake, bright bird ! and take
  Your fill of new-born rapture !
Wake lyre and lute, that erst were mute,
  Immortal strains to capture."

Ah ! then she rose whose deathless throes
  Of music thrilled the dawning :
Made young love seem a golden dream,
  Beneath Heav'n's sky-blue awning ;

And blithe she sped to rouse the dead
  From slumber to rejoicing ;
Then, sun-caressed, sank down to rest,
  Still " dawn " victorious voicing.

LOVE BEYOND LAW.

Do you still, my sweet, remember love's
awakening last September,
When I cast cold reason from me—when
I lost my soul for you ;
And I never thought of heeding, with your
soft eyes sadly pleading,
If the clouds were black above me, or the
sky was summer blue ?

Though bright days have dawned and perished
since the first hour that we cherished,
Though we've clambered cold to heaven,
and descended hot to hell,
Since two hearts went wildly beating with
the rapture of their meeting,
And our lips were loth to utter all that
eyes alone could tell ;

Though love ripened into passion in its
    helpless human fashion ;
Though we've sowed the seeds of folly, and
    the harvest is regret ;
Still, when even this has vanished with the
    past for ever banished,
'Tis the memory of that meeting that my
    heart can ne'er forget.

For your eyes were bright and burning with
    the fire of guilty yearning,
And I knew that love had conquered when
    their secret flashed in mine ;
And to each it little mattered if the universe
    were shattered,
For young love had clouded reason, and his
    madness was divine.

You were mine, past all redeeming, when your
    heart awoke from dreaming
In the sunrise of love's summer—in the
    springtime of delight ;
When warm passion kissed and crowned you,
    with the green leaves gathered round
    you,
And the day drooped into even, and the
    darkness drew the night.

You are mine, sweet flower, for ever, by those
    very ties we sever ;
  By that creed of cursed convention that our
    rebel hearts disdain.
In the spirit I shall take you, though my
    presence must forsake you,
  And our love shall live triumphant down
    dark hours of lonely pain.

LOVE, DEATH, AND SONG,
IN THRACE.

My little Lydian girl is dead;
Yet, ere she drooped her pretty head,
I brought white snowdrops to her bed,

And, in my grief, I whispered low :
" Ah ! stay, while yet thy sisters blow !
Stay, sweet ! I cannot let thee go."

She clasped and kissed the flowers I gave,
And said : " By Hebrus' rolling wave
Your snowdrop white will find a grave."

And once she faintly tried to sing ;
Then, sobbing like a stricken thing,
In gloom her soul went wandering.

I called her each endearing name—
(How cold they seemed !—my words, how
        tame !)—
No answer from the mute lips came.

54

All night I lay awake, and heard
The saddest song that ever stirred
The heart of man. No mortal bird

Hath power to flood the moon-kissed vale
With such a hopeless, haunting wail.
Ah ! soul-enchanting nightingale,

I know thee now : thou art my sweet :
'Twas thine—the passion-heart that beat
All night in music at my feet.

LOVE LAUGHS AT CASTE.

MERE money cannot wake warm love,
  That slumbers oft belated
In these sad days, nor millions move
  Two hearts once sweetly mated.

My Lady flaunts in silken gown,
  Or paints ; it little matters.
True love will go in russet brown
  To court true love in tatters.

Not silken sheen nor prudent paint,
  Nor modish styles of fashion,
Nor all the virtues of a saint,
  Can stir one spark of passion.

Mistress or maid—what matters it ?
  As mistress so the maid is.
Blue blood and birth count not a whit
  Where love the only trade is.

One woman with another vies
('Tis so throughout all ages) :
One at a marquis casts her eyes,
  Another at his pages.

But if his lordship should prefer
  The meaner rustic beauty,
And if his looks should light on her,
  What hinders love ?   Not duty.

The difference 'twixt that haughty dame,
  From every ill exempted,
And that poor girl without a name,
  Is this—that one was tempted.

LOVE, MORN, AND MUSIC.

OH ! give me love, with the trees above,
  In the dells where dewdrops cluster,
Heaven's heart of blue, and a trellised view
  Of morn's magnificent lustre,

And joy's bright bird in the clouds half heard,
  Or the cuckoo faintly calling,
Hushed happiness in the close caress
  Of passion that's never palling.

LOVE'S SILENT SHRINE.

WHERE once shone love, cold friendship ruled
    supreme,
And voices broke the silence of the shrine
That wist not of his solitude divine
Whose life passed from pursuing into dream :

From strenuous straining for a glimpse of
    truth,
From rushing river into memory's meres,
Into the calm of unforgotten years,
Into the golden granary of youth.

I knew what I had never known before—
The little light my friendship could bestow,
The coldness and the glamour of its glow,
Where love's imperious star flashed out of
    yore.

The loyal hearts of friends may count for
    much—
They throw faint starlight on the spirit's
    gloom :
But love can bring so many flowers to bloom,
To tremble into beauty at his touch !

For love can flood the universe with song,
And stir sweet strains of music out of sleep ;
Love sows the seeds that future thousands
    reap,
And makes the weakest arm supremely
    strong.

Love lures the hero soul to daring deed ;
Love conquers kingdoms for the sake of one ;
Love lends new rapture to the golden sun,
Mellows the moon, and fills with flowers the
    mead.

Love makes small souls gigantically rise,
And bid defiance to the shrinking world ;
Love dares, and tyrants, into Tartarus hurled,
Languish, and freedom's pinions cleave the
    skies.

But friendship cannot fill the throbbing hours
Of desolation with love's priceless boon,
So, from the memory of that afternoon,
I culled this little bunch of faded flowers.

No deep red roses of love's lost July,
No pinks to sanctify her maiden kiss,
No warm carnations of a wilder bliss,
To fill you with their sweetness where you lie,

Pensive perhaps, and lost to human view ;
Wrapt in the past, or living in the light
Of lofty thought. Ah ! sometimes let your
        sight
Fall on this little bunch of cornflowers blue.

NATURE'S SADNESS.

[*AFTER OLD ENGLISH.*]

ME soft-eyed sorrow courts
Where human grief is not,
And mournful Echo sports
Round that secluded grot
Where on green leaves I lie
And let the hours go by.

And Nature oft will bind
My soul with silent pain
For the sadness of the wind,
And the pathos of the rain,
And oft I shed a tear
For all dead flowers so dear.

I love the lilting lark,
The song that shatters sleep ;
But best the midnight dark,
With woe for words too deep ;
When the lorn nightingale's
Sweet sorrows flood the vales.

The ripple of the stream
Revealeth vain desire
To linger yet, and dream
By woodland glades afire
With yellow daffodils,
And cease awhile its rills.

The summer pines to stay
Among the forest leaves ;
But, on some dreary day,
Comes Autumn with his sheaves,
And green things grow to gold,
And canker with the cold.

The sunrise brings delight,
But the morn sheds pearls of dew
For the perished joys of night
And the stars she never knew ;
For the roses that *were* red ;
For the petals passion shed.

PASSION'S PASTORAL.

A STUPOR steals upon me ; I become
Like one who takes the magic of the moon
Too deeply in his veins to feel the sting
Of things ephemeral—one whose buoyant
    brain
Floats on thought's hasty tide to rapture's
    sea.
Now through me creeps delicious drowsiness
And calm content, as when some deity
Nods in Olympus o'er his nectar wine,
And folds the nymph he panted to possess
Unto his bosom. I would lay me down
Under the gloom of patriarchal oaks,
Snatching from solitude and jealous time
Some joy to gloat upon in darker years.
Woman's red lips, gold moonlight, and the
    gleam
And fair white contour of encircling arms,

In starlight's shadowless serenity,
Shall make my heaven ; while the nightingale
Hymns a sweet marriage service over us,
And bells our bridal forth from fluted throat.

SLEEP, DEAR!

THE night grows faint, like a swooning saint
    In the sight of the Holy Grail,
And the breeze, first born of the night and
      morn,
    Dies off in a plaintive wail :
    Then dream, dear! dream!
      Let never a gleam
From the shafts of sunrise find you,
Till vesper breathes o'er the crown love
      wreathes,
    And wild flowers freshly bind you.

The long grass shakes in the leafy brakes
    When the golden light appears,
And earth, like a bride half-terrified,
    Smiles up through a veil of tears :

Then sleep, dear! sleep!
Lest the sun-god leap
From the shameless east, and find you
With cheeks all flushed for the joys that
blushed
In the burning hours behind you.

SONG.

COME to my arms, O sweet!
The world, enchanted, dreams,
In summer heat of passion's feet,
And Luna's amorous beams.

Come to my arms, O sweet!
The tireless wings of Time
Shall stay their flight where the love-
    sick night
Droops warm on a cloudless clime.

She comes to my arms—my sweet,
Moon-kissed and wind-caressed.
The love-light lies in her starry eyes,
And—Nature knows the rest.

SONNET.

FRONTED with fate, and knowing he must
    die,
Whose gush of gore encrimsons all the grass,
Life's little shiftings scened before him pass—
The solemn world of childish fantasy :
Passion's superb red sunrise in youth's sky,
And, scarcely with a tear for what he was,
Stricken in manhood's strength he droops,
    alas !
And doffs the tatters of mortality,
With laughter on his lips : his latest breath
A prayer that truth may triumph in the light,
And dissolution only quickeneth
The soul that never yielded to affright ;
That scorns the shadowy terrors of dim death,
And with firm footfall beats the blinding
    night.

THEE ONLY.

When all my nights are lonely,
  And all my days are long,
My thoughts turn to thee only,
  And bind thy brows with song :
    For all the flowers
    Of lyric hours
  To thee alone belong.

When all my heart is aching
  For woes I cannot heal,
When sunless dawns are waking,
  To thee alone I kneel :
    Through clouds and cares
    My broken prayers
  To thy dear bosom steal.

Thy face alone I cherish,
  When other faces fade ;
When loves ephemeral perish,
  And idols are unmade.
    Of all bereft,
    So thou art left,
  I shall not be afraid.

THE GUARDIAN OF THE FOUNT.

AT the fount of the Muses a dragon lies
    dreaming,
    And no man may drink of the wonderful
    wave
But he conquer the foe with his sword and
    lance gleaming.
    The magic of song is the meed of the
    brave.

'Tis the fiend of affright that lies watching
    these waters—
    Foul dragon, thrice-coiled round the well-
    springs of song,
Who guards the pure stream of Mnemosyne's
    daughters,
    And none may approach save the fearless
    and strong.

For malice and hate follow after the seeker
  Whom fiend could not conquer, nor terror
    control ;
His sabre smites keen for the wounded, the
    weaker,
  But tempests shall tirelessly rage round his
    soul.

I crave but a drop from the silver-tongued
    eddy :
  This drained, I will hie me right joyously
    home,
Singing : " Soldier of Truth, in the ranks ever
    ready,
  God's starlight is shrouded, but morning
    shall come."

THE SEER.

Love seems more fair for lonely hours of
    sorrow,
And darkness lends more rapture to the
    light.
The day would drag and weary without
    morrow,
And sleepless suns might sicken for the
    night.

Not all in gloom, nor yet in light eternal,
    We wend our way to where God's ocean
    rolls :
Still winter lingers, though the vales grow
    vernal,
    And storms await to vex too venturous
    souls.

Yet, though the singer sees but gloom sur-
round him ;
Though venom's bitter tongue tries to
defame ;
His sword still seeks the countless hosts around
him,
Smites for the truth, and puts them all to
shame.

And some far-distant sun shall gleam and
gladden
The brow of him who prophesied the
day ;
Though doubt distract, though shaft of
slander sadden,
And Martyr's thorns are mingled with the
bay,

His eyes shall view the promised land, that
never
His feet may tread who served God's people
well ;
His deathless name endure with us for ever
Who fought for truth, and in the conflict
fell ;

And generation call to generation,—
  " Lo ! this is he who sang the dawn between
Dark midnight hours, when no light brought
    salvation.
    Peace to his ashes !   Keep his memory
    green."

Aye ! though vast tracts of darkness close
    behind him,
  Though earth receives the blood he freely
    shed,
God's meed upon the mountain-top shall find
    him,
  And all the pomp of sunrise crown his head.

The world shall live more lovely for his being
  Whose grand, imperious spirit drew the
    morn
From sombre skies ; who, victory far foreseeing,
  Bequeathed his sword to warrior souls un-
    born.

TO AN OLD-WORLD LOVE.

SWEET old-world love, on whose soft locks
 descending—
Gold upon gold—the sunbeams used to
 play,
By day, by night, with pity passion
 blending,
Thy starry eyes illume my lonely
 way.

When Time, who brings no bedfellow but
 sorrow,
And loveless years, have done their worst
 to chill
The drooping soul that shuns the sad to-
 morrow,
And darkling thoughts are boding some
 new ill,

Thy phantom form shines through the dark-
    ness o'er me ;
  Shatters the chains that held me, helpless
    bound ;
And long-lost days of rapture rise before
    me
  When by thy love my soul was clasped
    around.

" *Was* clasped," said I ?   Nay ! love endures
    for ever :
  'Tis this that keeps me sane, that goads
    me on.
My guiding-star, were I from thee to
    sever,
  Life would be death, or death be dear
    alone.

Yet, as it is, love calls me to my duty,
  Though thou art gone, 'tis only for a
    time.
Still through the dark the loadstone of thy
    beauty
  Draws on my soul from height to height
    to climb.

So I will not complain, but bear me boldly,
  Nor stress of storm shall drive me from
    my post ;
And though the stars may shine upon me
    coldly,
  In some far world I'll find the love I lost.

TO L. G. A.

A HEART that beats along the barren years
Alone, unloved, that only friendship cheers,
But cannot soothe when desolation fills
The empty creeks that love has never laved :
A heart whose only prayer is peace, that
      stills,
And broods upon dim eyes, and broken wills
That in pride's Nessus shirt the world have
      braved,—

This heart, so human in its helplessness,
And so inhuman under fiery stress
Of scathing malice and the mark that brands
The son of song, however frail he be,
Salutes you with these poppies for your
      hands ;
Some gathered in green meads and antique
      lands,
Some by the gloom-robed, ever-restless sea.

These withered flowers are all I can bestow :
I may not linger where the roses grow,
Nor in some smiling valley take my rest ;
But you, with tuneful inspiration sweet,
Have drawn the sting of sorrow from my
      breast,
And lightened of the load that on me
      pressed :
Then take this little tribute at your feet.

TO NATURE.

OH! many a time upon thy kind old breast
I've eased my heart of persecution's quest,
And, gazing awestruck over solemn skies,
Sunk swooning into mystic reveries;
And often, when the bitter tears were blinding,
I've felt thy gentle arms around me winding,
And heard a zephyr whisper in mine ear :
" Child of the sun and sea, thy home is here.
Where in the brake the fluted throstles sing,
And homing doves are faintly hovering,
Calm peace shall lay what human anguish
     lingers,
And sweep the lyre with mild, angelic fingers.
Then take thy wounded spirit from the world
To where the heart of Nature is unfurled;
Where, o'er thy head, the trembling tree-tops
    close,
And life is one long summer of repose,

By star-kissed stream, and echo-haunted cave,
And lonely isle that lazy waters lave ;
Where sorrow sleeps, and all existence seems
A many-coloured galaxy of dreams."

WHERE ARE YOU NOW?

SWEET! where are you now?
Do the wanton sunbeams, glancing,
Kiss those queenly eyes entrancing?
    Light that lovely brow?

Sweet! what fancies blow,
What thrice happy breezes, round you?
Only this—that love has found you:
    This alone I know.

Sweet! where'er you be,
Love shall lead my heart to follow,
As, in search of sun, the swallow
    Skims the rocking sea.

Sweet! how fares my heart?
Do the dainty lips that stole it
In the silent hours console it
    For the leagues that part?

Let my days be drear!
Grief of small account I'll reckon.
All night long bright visions beckon :
Darkness draws us near.

THE BRIDE OF LIFE.

IN dreams my spirit found her
  Star-driven, rapture-led ;
Night's quivering coils crept round her,
  And with the dawn she fled.
I dreamed that love had crowned her
  With roses newly dead.

She haunts me to undoing,
  This Lady of my quest ;
Through midnight hours pursuing
  I seek a sheltering breast ;
That yields not to my wooing
  Its secret unconfessed.

Calm sentinel of slumbers,
  Nor wearying she stands ;
Yet calls in noiseless numbers,
  And holds seductive hands,
To where the clay encumbers
  My soul in iron bands.

Old loves have been before her,
  And seared with ardent breath
The heart that doth implore her,
  That thrills, and quickeneth
Cold passion to adore her
  Whose maiden name is Death.

CAROL NO MORE.

Too loud she sings her new-born happiness.
O hush thee, swallow-heart, upon thy way!
For yonder clouds are boding of distress,
And darkness smites the day.

Too loud, too clear
Thy carols arise,
For the night is near
With her lullabies;
She shall hush to sleep
Thy fluttering soul,
With the lightning's sweep
And the thunder-roll;
She shall follow and find
Thy secret pain
With the watch-dog wind
And the shepherd rain.

The sun shall slope
O'er the red, red sea,
And gossamer Hope
With soiled wings flee.
Too clear, too loud
Thy carols arise :
Fate is weaving a shroud
O'er the glimmering skies ;
Fate is digging a tomb
For a dainty form
In the gathered gloom
Of the rising storm.

BEYOND WORDS.

I WORSHIP thee beyond my words can tell,
And all sweet thoughts at thought of thee
    take birth :
These flowers I gathered from the grand old
    earth,
But one stray bud I deemed from Heaven
    fell.

And if this be, and thou wilt call it thine,
Though Faith be coy, and Hope a fickle jade,
Of thy great Charity, sweetheart, be mine,
And with thy light illume a singer's shade.

OF HIS MUSE.

No vision of inglorious years of gloom,
Nor Lethe's flood that laps a sunken soul,
Can break her tideless billows to control.
Oh she was cradled in the fiery womb
Of giant forces, swathed at Summer's loom,
And rocked to sleep by Autumn's thunder-
    roll ;
She drained the mother-milk of Winter's bowl,
And with the Spring rejoicing rent the tomb.

If through the tenour of her course there
    dreams
A gentle surge of lightly shaken leaves,
The silver strain of unpolluted streams,
A scent of Shiraz where she waits and weaves
Through songlit hours her many-chorded
    themes,
The promise of her birth my Muse achieves.

THE LIGHT OF DEATH.

SLOWLY o'er the sunken face
Pallid-grey the shades are sweeping,
As upon the day comes creeping
    Night's mysterious twilight grace.

Softly, as the shadows fall
When the spectral light has wended,
Where the white and black are blended
    Into eve's uncertain pall,

So, upon life's tragic day,
Gleam of rapture, gloom of sorrow,
Steals a night without a morrow
    In the quivering deathlight grey.

Who can track him to his goal?
Where the light in shadow merges
Is there peace upon life's verges?
    Is there starshine on his soul?

WHAT REMAINS.

In a desolate shrine,
And a harp that is hushed,
There's a trace of the wine
And the music that gushed,
Though the hand of the priest
Brings oblations no more,
And the numbers have ceased
That enchanted of yore.

So my heart has a stain
Of the dregs of delight,
And a sullen refrain
Haunts the hag-ridden night.
Not a tribute of tears
Ever falls, and the moan
Of the music that sears
Is a song of my own.

A FALLEN DEITY.

OH, it was pitiful to see this man,
So starlike once, now humbled in the dust
Of swinish craving, and insatiate lust—
The ruined lineaments of youth to scan,
O'er which the demon Drink had placed her
    ban :
With watery eyes, and clawing hands out-
    thrust,
Beating the air, to beg a paltry crust,
And all the while his tuneful numbers ran,

And inspiration babbled at the fount
Of broken godhead.   As he strove to mount
His jaded Pegasus, unbidden tears
Rose at the sight of genius in a stye ;
Then a mad whirl of mocking thoughts went
    by,
And in their track the dark-browed phantom
    years.

ON READING "FROM DAWN TO SUNSET."

I KNOW not what grand voice of ecstasy
Rang through the shuddering caverns of
  despair,
Wresting the monster Madness from his lair,
And bade the rebel-soul of Rancour—die,
Bringing to Doubt the balm of sympathy,
The kiss of Peace to heavy-hearted Care,
Smoothed Sorrow's wrinkled brow and tangled
  hair
With its most human haunting melody.

But this I know—a stone was rolled away
That barred my shrouded being from the day,
And down the gloom God's herald light sped
  fast.
Then from the womb of Death I sprang, and
  cried :
" I live—I live, who once was crucified,"
And into sunlight, singing, rose at last.

THE POET'S LEGACY.

WHEN this—that once was I—is void of
    breath,
And on my lips the leaden lips of Death
Are softly pressed, and Nature's close embrace
Has kissed the tell-tale furrows from my
    face ;
When Time has set his seal upon these brows,
And passion's melted into memory's drowse ;
When o'er the broken harp's tear-sodden
    strings
Sad Muses droop their unavailing wings ;
When other cares have taught thee to forget
The star that made one night divine, and set
In stormy splendour on the sullen track,
O'er death's abysmal sea of vasty black ;—
The voice I leave behind shall hale thee back,
And bid thee gaze above the giddy throng
On thine own woman-heart enshrined in song.

SUDDEN LIGHT.

A GLEAM of light, a vision of sunshine caught
    me,
Beat back the gloom for the term of a
    golden hour ;
White arms enclosed, and wild lips suddenly
    sought me,
And out of my heart there burst a glorious
    flower—
A rose of song that had blossomed and
    dawned to beauty,
Through throbbing nights and the drench
    of passionate tears ;
Whose crimson heart was the life-blood shed
    for duty,
Whose barren thorns were the unrejoicing
    years.
A balm there was of a summer of all sweet
    summers,
A scent of surfeited Mays of moonless bliss ;

When love seemed real to her passion-
    prompted mummers,
And history hung on their first enraptured
    kiss ;
When the breathless night was still, and the
    stars had covered
Their conscious eyes, and never a murmur
    broke
The swoon of the slumberous spell that faintly
    hovered
O'er dreamlit dales where only a Zephyr
    spoke—
O'er the forest where glimmered in gloom
    cathedral arches,
Mysterious aisles, and whispering porticoes,
With ghostly columns of shadowy spectral
    larches,
Where God endures as a Spirit of vast repose.

TO EURYDICE.

WORDS, not deeds, are idle—idle :
   Only action is divine.
Every bard must have his bridle :
   I have mine.

Yet if words could find fruition
   On whatever soil they fell,
Save one spirit from perdition—
   It is well.

If some single lyric, straying,
   Find an echo in your breast,
Of the hours I've spent a-maying,
   One is blest.

If a song have power to tear you
   From this vast and voiceless gloom ;
Then, by Heaven ! I'll win and wear you
   Until doom.

THE MAIDEN'S VIGIL.

In my fancy sings a maiden
  By the barren moonlit shore,
Where the sea for ever surges,
  And the wild storm-furies roar ;
Wailing weird funereal dirges
  From a heart that hopes no more.

In my dreams I see her lifting
  Tearless eyes across the gloom ;
Round her soul the tempest, mocking,
  Shrieks the sailor's chant of doom :
At her feet the billows, rocking,
  Roll their dull receding boom.

And the winds and waters, chiding,
  Bid her nightly vigil keep :
With the lone heart overladen,
  And the eyes that never weep,
Thou shalt be for ever, maiden,
  Moaning dirges by the deep."

FAREWELL!

BE brave, my sweet, look up and say : " Fare-
  well ! "—
The last sad word that I may hear you speak;
For love so mighty, human will so weak,
My own voice chills me like a tolling bell,
Rolls in my breast its cold continuous knell,
And rings the ready teardrops down my
  cheek.
Then say the word that I so vainly seek
To cast across love's ever-surging swell.

We part in passion still unsatisfied,
Leaving the sunlit shores of hope behind :
You with the snow-white canvas of a bride,
And I with bare poles bending to the
  wind.
Be mine the ocean heart of lonely pride,
And yours the soul that tyrants cannot
  bind.

WORLD-WEARY.

SHE had murmured adieu to laughter,
  She had waved to mirth on the wing,
And youth with a sigh went after
  The innocent hours of spring.
May vanished, and, crimson-hearted,
  Rose June upon dream-flushed skies :
Love shattered the clouds, and parted
  The mist from her maiden eyes.

Through summer he spake and thrilled
      her,
  And many a passion seared
Ere the kisses of autumn chilled her
  And blighted the hopes once reared.
Love's damascene rose now faded,
  Yet languishes undesired,
Where her beautiful soul beams jaded,
  Through eyes world-weary and tired.

NO HEART BUT THINE.

HE has no heart but thine wherein to rest ;
He brings no gems to consecrate that shrine ;—
But, of whatever in him is divine
    Take thou the best.

Men only know him as he seems ; yet thou
Shalt hear faint prophecies of fame, and mark
The feet of sunrise moving through the dark.
Oh ! come, sweet pilot of a lonely bark,
    Not then, but now.

SONG WITHOUT ECHO.

[*FROM THE POLISH OF MARIE KONOPNICKA.*]

HEIGHO! shades are creeping :
Heigho! storms are sweeping :
Heigho, shadows quiver
Hiding all your path from view, dear :
Heigho! runs the river,
Carried by the tempest flying :
Heigho! my heart goes crying,
Down the track that leads to you, dear.

As the sun sweeps mountain-passes,
Over meres and meadow-grasses,
So my fate was fain to follow
With the sun-rejoicing swallow.
Ah, my fate! whom storms have parted,
Cradled in the forest bosom—
Flowerlike fate, you do not blossom
Where spring dallies, April-hearted.

You have left the woodlands lonely,
Left a starless sky above me,
Given grief's caresses only,
Only sorrow's lips to love me.
Not for me the warm delights
Smiling from dear lanes and valleys ;
But o'er a stranger's roof o' nights
A song without an echo sallies.
Oh ! not for me that homestead fair
Gleams among dim vistas lying ;
But o'er a stranger's roof Despair
Wails a dirge for ever dying.

SHOULD THEY ASK.

Should they ask you : " Where is he
Of the simple, foolish mind,
And the harp that sang of summer when no
    leaf was on the tree ? "
Will you say he's gone in chase
Of a far-off phantom face,
Of a quarry that eludes him, and a love he
    cannot find.

Should they ask you for the wight,
Whom your wise ones held in scorn :
Will you say he's gone a-gliding down the
    dark stream of the night,
Seeking ever what is lost,
With his wild heart tempest-tost,
Through a sea of starless horror to a shadow-
    land forlorn.

SLEEPER AND SENTINEL.

THE wind sings loud
O'er the snow-white shroud
That covers her breast,
Who lies caressed
By the hand of sleep in the lap of rest.
But he gives no heed
If the storm recede,
Or snows and sleet
On his eyelids beat,
Who watches white as a winding-sheet ;
For he stands alone,
Unloved, unknown,
O'er the grave of a heart that was once
his own.

LOVE'S WITNESS.

I CREEP to the window softly
   This joyous night in June,
But the strings of my heart's wild harping
   Are frayed and out of tune.
Night's mild-eyed mystical Goddess
   Steals over the silver grass,
And down by the dim laburnums
   Two happy lovers pass.

Ah! little they know who watches
   The path where shadow lies,
A sneer on his shapeless features,
   And hate in his hollow eyes.
Though the summer night is golden,
   There's a form the doomed ones miss—
Grim Death by the willows waiting
   To sever the lips that kiss.

But Peace upon calm creation
  Sits brooding as a dove,
And the mother-heart is throbbing
  In unison with love.
Yet I, being many-sided,
  Shall lone and loveless be,
Till the wan moon wanes for ever,
  And the stars are drowned at sea.

VITA BREVIS.

[*FROM THE FRENCH OF DE MUSSET.*]

So fleet is life :
A little scope
For heart and hope,
A little strife,
  And then :—Good-day !

A few bright gleams
Of pleasure brief,
A passing grief,
Some broken dreams—
  Good-night ! Away !

L'ENVOI.

TO GEORGE BARLOW.

I CARE not a straw for approval
  (Fame's trumpet too often is tin)
Of the cliques and the critics, since you've all
  The praise I would perish to win.

Dame Fortune, sweet wanton, is fickle ;
  Yet though she caressingly smile
On some desperate effort to tickle
  The popular palate by guile,

Oh ! believe 'tis not for the favour
  Of those who can make me or damn
That my songs of the fields have a savour,
  And my lyre breathes a hatred of sham.

Oh ! believe me, 'tis not for the dollars,
  Nor yet for the pleasures they bring,
That the meanest of Poesy's scholars
  Would follow her fugitive wing.

For the joys of the forest are sweeter :
　New treasures will gladden his eyes
Who has worshipped his Mother Demeter
　Where among the green meadows she lies.

'Tis the privilege born of pursuing
　Truth's beacon that lures him along ;
'Tis the right of love's passionate wooing
　To lighten the heart with a song.

Let the Pharisee snivel, and squander
　His choicest abuse on my name,
Or the Philistine fearfully ponder
　On one who is heedless of shame.

But in meanness and malice they revel :
　Their opinion is nothing to me ;
So the *bourgeois* may go to the devil,
　Like the Gadarene swine to the sea.

Printed by Hazell, Watson, & Viney, Ld., London and Aylesbury.

Press Opinions

POEMS BY "PAGANUS."

"We are fain to stop and stay awhile at the rhymes of 'Paganus,' the poems as usual commanding special attention."—*Glasgow Echo.*

"The poetical contributions, of which there are several, are all of high merit. A true ring marks the contributions of 'Paganus.'"—*Belfast Weekly Telegraph.*

"The verse is of a high order of merit."—*Perthshire Advertiser.*

"A very pretty set of verses by 'Paganus.'"—*Pall Mall Gazette.*

"The satirical verse is good."—*Cambrian.*

"The poetry, too, is far and away beyond the average."—*Book and News Trade Gazette.*

"Some very charming poems."—*Weekly Irish Times.*

"The 'Sex Militant' is very good indeed."—*Lady's Pictorial.*

"Verse of good quality."—*Liverpool Daily Post.*

"'Paganus,' too, can write poetry."—*North Devon Herald.*

Etc., Etc., Etc.

Telegraphic Address: 'QUILLDRIVER, LONDON."

Cablegrams: "A.B.C." CABLE CODE.

Cheques to be crossed

The London Joint Stock Bank, Limited.

A SELECTION FROM THE

List of Publications,

TOGETHER WITH SOME PRESS OPINIONS OF THE AUTHORS' PREVIOUS OR PRESENT WORKS.

ISSUED BY

THE ROXBURGHE PRESS,

CONDUCTED BY

MR. CHARLES F. RIDEAL,

Fellow of the Royal Society of Literature, etc.

LONDON:

3, VICTORIA STREET, WESTMINSTER,

where all Communications should be Addressed.

RETAIL AT

32, CHARING CROSS, S.W.

Trade Agents:

MESSRS.

SIMPKIN, MARSHALL, HAMILTON, KENT & Co., Limited.

TO AUTHORS.

Cbe Roxburgbe Press undertake the printing and publishing of approved MSS. in all departments of Literature on a basis of actual cost. Estimates supplied Free. The Publishing Department is specially arranged for the purpose of advantageously bringing Books before the Trade, the Libraries, and the Public. No secret profits are indulged in. Accounts are settled upon the certificate of a Chartered Accountant, and everything is done to promote the interests of Authors and their works.

"For dainty book-work commend us to the Roxburghe Press. Everything turned out by this high-class house is of the very best description. Good taste and a thorough appreciation of the beautiful characterises all their publications."—*Bolton Evening Echo.*

AGENCIES IN

THE UNITED STATES, CANADA, AFRICA, AUSTRALIA, INDIA, AND THE CONTINENT

1895.

CONTENTS.

INDEX OF SUBJECTS.

3

INDEX OF SUBJECTS (*continued*)

LIST OF AUTHORS, ARTISTS, ETC.

LIST OF AUTHORS, ARTISTS, ETC.

(*continued*).

SCIENTIFIC,

GENERAL,

TRAVEL,

REMINISCENCE

FICTION.

ACROSS THE ATLANTIC. By R. ANDERTON
NAYLOR, F.R.S.Lit., Author of "Nugæ Canoræ,"
etc. Presentation Edition.
"Bright, interesting, beautifully produced."—*Th Institute.*

WOMAN REGAINED. A Study of Passion. A
Novel of Artistic Life. By GEORGE BARLOW. Six
Shillings. [*Shortly.*
"There is much splendid versification in THE CRUCIFIXION OF
MAN."—*Glasgow Herald.*
"The new volume is essentially the work of a poet , . . his force it
is impossible not to recognise."—*Literary World.*
"All will read it with sustained interest. Mr. Barlow is to be con
gratulated on his work."—*Vanity Fair.*
"The most striking volume of poetry we have read for many a day
In the first rank of modern poetry. Let every student of life read
this work of genius."—*Scots Magazine.*

**THE REMINISCENCES OF A SEPTUAGEN-
ARIAN CITIZEN.** By EDWARD CALLOW. Large
paper edition, limited to 250 copies, specially bound,
numbered, and signed by Author. Illustrated, 21s.
net. [*In Preparation.*
"The 'Phynodderee,' an interesting collection of Manx legends,
has been presented to the Queen and the Prince of Wales, and graciously accepted by those illustrious personages. It is difficult to
speak critically of a book which has received so high an *imprimatur.*
The stories have a genuine ring about them."—*Athenæum.*
"In this well-mounted volume Mr. Callow essays the same labour
of love on behalf of beautiful Mona that Lady Charlotte Guest and
Mr. Siles have performed between them for the land of the Cymry.
—*Globe.*

EVOLUTION, A RETROSPECT. The (slightly
revised) Address delivered before the Royal British
Association at Oxford 1894. By the MARQUIS OF
SALISBURY, K.G., etc. Cloth, Eighteenpence net ;
Post Free 3*d.* extra.

THE RE-UNION OF CHRISTENDOM. The
(revised, with an Introduction and Appendix)
Address delivered before the Conference under the
auspices of the Catholic Truth Society at Preston
1894, by His Eminence CARDINAL VAUGHAN, Arch-
bishop of Westminster. Cloth, Eighteenpence net ;
Post Free 3*d.* extra.

**A BIBLIOGRAPHY OF GUNS AND SHOOT-
ING.** Being a List of Ancient and Modern English
and Foreign Books Relating to Firearms and their
Use, and to the Composition and Manufacture of
Explosives; with an Introductory Chapter on
Technical Books and the Writers of them, Firearms
Inventions and the History of Gunmaking, and the
Development of the Art of Wing Shooting. By
WIRT GERRARE, formerly Editor of *The Gun-
maker,The Sporting Goods Review,* etc., etc. 10s. 6*d.*
net; Post Free. Buckram. A Limited Edition.

SPORTING PERIODICALS — PSEUDONYMS.

Being a Guide to the British, Colonial, and Foreign Newspapers, Reviews, and Technical Periodicals, which Treat of Guns and Shooting; with an Index to Sporting Articles in other Publications, and a List of the Pseudonyms used by Sportsmen. By WIRT GERRARE, Author of "A Bibliography of Guns and Shooting," formerly Editor of *The Sporting Goods Review*, etc., etc. This Guide will be to the past and current periodical literature of Guns and Shooting what the "Bibliography" is to published books. It will contain particulars of every Sporting Newspaper and every Technical Service Periodical. In addition to Publishers' Addresses, the information given will comprise many notices of Editors and chief Contributors, thus constituting the work a Practical Dictionary of the Sporting Press; therefore indispensable to Writers, Publishers, Gunmakers, and such Students of the Technical Literature of Guns and Shooting. Uniform with the "Bibliography of Guns and Shooting." Demy 8vo, 10s. 6d. net, Post Free.

[In Preparation.

A GLOSSARY AND POLYGLOT DICTIONARY

OF TECHNICAL WORDS AND IDIOMS Used in the Firearms Industry, together with Records, Tables, Formulæ, Tests, and Descriptions of some of the Gauging and Measuring Instruments used in Proving of Firearms. By WIRT GERRARE, Contributor to "Murray's Dictionary," Author of "A Bibliography of Guns and Shooting," formerly Editor of *The Gunmaker*, etc., etc., etc. The Contents comprise : A Complete Glossary of Technical Words and Phrases, with Exact Definitions, and the Equivalent Technical Names or Idioms in French, German, Italian, Spanish, and in many cases in Swedish and Russian also ; Comparative Tables of English and Foreign Weights and Measures in use in the Firearms Trade. Formulæ for Computing Pressures in Foot Pounds and Atmospheres ; Rules for Estimating Velocities and Penetration ; Records of Shot Guns and Rifles ; Descriptions of Chronometers, Velocimeters, and other Instruments for Ascertaining Shooting Power. Targets, Ranges, and Technical Information concerning Explosives and Projectiles. This book therefore is indispensable to all Students of Techniques, to all who write of Guns and Shooting, and to all who are interested in the Firearms Trade, whether as Manufacturers or Dealers.

[In Preparation.

THE MAGISTRACY. Being a Directory and Biographical Dictionary of the Justices of the Peace of the United Kingdom. Edited by Charles F. Rideal. 21s. [*In Preparation.*

THE SENATE. A Review of Modern and Progressive Thought. Edited by L. Cranmer-Byng and C. Gordon Winter. Published on the First of each Month, Sixpence. Subscription, 7s. 6d. per annum, post free.

"Truly the thanks of all men are due to such reformers as the conductors of this frank and fearless organ. The prose is excellent . . . poetry . . . good, particularly 'Love beyond Law,' by Paganus."—*The Australian Trading World.*

". . . It is as well got up as anything of its kind need be."—*Vanity Fair.*

". . . It is . . . the organ of two bright young men."—*Manchester Guardian.*

THE IDEA OF A PATRIOT PARTY. By A. Egmont Hake, with Contributions by L. Cranmer-Byng, O. E. Wesslau and F. Fletcher-Vane. 16s. ; Post Free 6d. extra. [*In Preparation.*

INDIA IN NINE CHAPTERS. By A. M. O. Richards. One Shilling ; Post Free 3d. extra.

"Will go a long way towards encouraging the tourists to visit India."—*Western Mail.*

"A considerable amount of compressed information."—*Chimes Corner.*

"TOLD AT THE CLUB." Some Short Stories. Being No. 1 of the " Potboiler " Series. By Charles F. Rideal. Manilla, Eighteenpence, Cloth Half-a-crown ; Post Free 3d. extra. [*In preparation*

MANDRAKES. Original Stories of Some Unregarded Items. By Wirt Gerrare, Author of " Phantasms," "Rufin's Legacy," etc., etc. A Time Limited Edition. Crown 8vo, cloth, 3s. 6d. [*In Preparation.*

WOMEN OF THE TIME : Being a Dictionary of Biographical Records of Eminent Women of the Day. Revised to date, and edited by Charles F. Rideal (Fellow of the Royal Society of Literature). Demy 8vo, cloth. Fourteen Shillings. [*In Preparation.*

11

PICTURES FROM A BLOOMSBURY BOARD-
ING HOUSE (Illustrated). By CHARLES F. RIDEAL.
[In Preparation

DRY TOAST. Some thoughts upon some subjects
not generally dealt with. By CHARLES F. RIDEAL.

Contents :—A Piece of the Crust; Brains and Black
Butter; On the Mending of Bellows; On Backbone,
or rather the Want of it; Some Phases of Modern
Honesty; On Giving Advice—and Taking it; Concerning "Hums"; On Flap-Doodle—the Thick and
the Thin; On "Cranks"; On the Art of Making
Oneself Uncomfortable; On Pouring Cold Water;
On Always Doing Something; Some of the Advan-
tages of being Religious ; On Playing One's Cards;
On Living it Down; On Friendship; On Fame;
etc., etc.

[In Preparation.

PEOPLE WE MEET. By CHARLES F. RIDEAL.
Illustrated by HARRY PARKES. Second and Revised Edition. One Shilling ; Post Free 3*d.* extra.

" A series of really amusing sketches of familiar types of ladies and
gentlemen with whom most of us come into frequent contact."—
Public Opinion.

" Twenty-four clever and characteristic sketches of types o. people
to be met with in and out of society.   Each fancy portrait is accom-
panied by a few lines of explanatory or descriptive letterpress, which
is in perfect accord with the individual portrayed.   If readers have
not met them all, they will at least recognise some of them, though,
perhaps, they may not be desirous of renewing their acquaintance."—
Morning Post.

Author and artist seem to have got on well together."—*Punch.*

A collection of characteristic sketches drawn with much humou
and crisply described."—*Scotsman.*

A ROMANCE OF THE FAIR, and other Short
Stories. By L. and H. CRANMER-BYNG. Manilla,
Eighteenpence ; Cloth, Half-a-crown ; Post Free,
3*d.* extra. *[In Preparation*

THE SENATE EXTRAS. No. 1.
Pyjama Purists," by CHARLES F. RIDEAL, and
'Virtue Made Easy," by H. C. B.
Price Two-pence. Post Free, ½*d.* extra.

DICKENSIANA.

'**WELLERISMS**," from "Pickwick" and "Master Humphrey's Clock." Selected by CHARLES F. RIDEAL, and Edited with an Introduction by CHARLES KENT, Author of "The Humour and Pathos of Charles Dickens." Third Edition. With a new and original drawing by GEORGE CRUIK-SHANK, JUNR., of Mr. Samuel Weller. Manilla, Eighteenpence; Cloth, Half-a-crown; Post Free 3*d*. extra.

Contents: — Sam Weller's Introduction; Old Weller at Doctor's Commons; Sam on a Legal Case; Self-acting Ink; Out with it; Sam's Old White Hat; Independent Voters; Proud o' the Title; The Weller Philosophy; The Twopenny Rope; Job Trotter's Tears; Sam's Misgivings as to Mr. Pickwick; Clear the Way for the Wheelbarrow; Unpacking the Lunch Hamper; Battledore and Shuttlecock; a True Londoner; Spoiling the Beadle; Old Weller's Remedy for the Gout; Sam on Cabs; Poverty and Oysters; Old Weller on "Pikes"; Sam's Power of Suction; Veller and Gammon; Sam as Master of the Ceremonies; Sam before Mr. Nupkins; Sam's Introduction to Mary and the Cook; Something behind the Door; Sam and Master Bardell; Good Wishes to Messrs. Dodson and Fogg; Sam and His Mother-in-Law; The Shepherd's Water Rates; Stiggins as an Arithmetician; Sam and the Fat Boy; Compact and Comfortable; Apologue of the Fat Man's Watch; Medical Students; Sam Subpœnaed; Disappearance of the "Sausage" Maker; Sam Weller's Valentine; Old Weller's Plot; Tea Drinking at Brick Lane; The Soldier's Evidence Inadmissible; Sam's "Wision" Limited; A Friendly "Swarry"; The Killebeate; Sam and the Surly Groom; Mr. Pickwick's Dark Lantern; The Little Dirty-faced Man; Old Weller Inexorable; Away with Melancholy; Post Boys and Donkeys; A Vessel: Old Weller's Threat; Sam's Dismissal of the Fat Boy; Is She a Widder? Bill Blinder's Request; The Watch-box Boy.

THE LAW AND LAWYERS OF PICKWICK

(With an Original Sketch of "Mr. Serjeant Buzfuz"). By Sir FRANK LOCKWOOD, Q.C., M.P. Second Edition, slightly revised. Manilla, One Shilling. Cloth, a veritable Edition de Luxe, Eighteenpence net; Post Free 3d. extra.

" The lecture itself is full of that genial humour characteristic of Mr. Lockwood, who is acknowledged to be the most jocular of Queen's Counsellors, and the cleverest caricaturist at the Bar. He has been a devoted student of the works of Charles Dickens, and has selected with much discrimination those passages that most strikingly exhibit the novelist's acquaintance with legal men and affairs fifty years ago."—*Dundee Advertiser.*

" The effort was well worthy of permanent inclusion in Dickensian ore, and, as it is published at the price of one shilling, the little brochure is likely to find an extended field of readers. It is prefaced by an original pen and ink sketch of Serjeant Buzfuz by Mr. Lockwood, who is, as is generally known, an adept at characteristic portraiture of this kind."—*Umpire.*

CHARLES DICKENS' HEROINES AND

WOMEN FOLK: Some thoughts concerning them. A Revised Lecture. By CHARLES F. RIDEAL, with Drawings of "Dot" and "Edith Dombey.' Second Edition, Cloth, Two Shillings; Post Free 3d. extra.

A delightful little book."—*Institute.*

VERSE

AND

SONG.

POEMS OF PAGANISM; OR, SONGS OF LIFE
AND LOVE. By "PAGANUS." Six Shillings
Post Free, 3d. extra.

[In preparation.

"The satirical verse is good."—*Cambrian.*

"Paganus too can write poetry."—*North Devon Herald.*

"'Love beyond Law' calling for especial praise."—*Popular Medi
cal Monthly.*

THE MOUNTAIN LAKE AND OTHER POEMS.
From the works of FRIEDRICH VON BODENSTEDT
Translated by JULIA PRESTON. Antique paper,
daiotily bound, Six Shillings ; Post Free, 3d. extra.
A Limited Edition.

"Her Majesty The Queen has been graciously pleased to accept
a copy of the book."—*Extract from Letter from the Right Hon. Sir
Henry Ponsonby.*

"Many of the verses embody beautiful ideas,"—*Bucks Herald.*

HOMER'S WINE AND OTHER POEMS. By
LAURA G. ACKROYD. Six Shillings ; Post Free,
3d. extra. *[In Preparation.*

It is interesting to notice Miss Ackroyd's conclusions."—*Literar
World.*

"I had been struck with a ew verses quoted in her letter, and that
I would gladly read some more."—*Golden Gates.*

SHAKESPEARE'S SONGS AND SONNETS;
together with his Lyrics and Verse. Selected
by EDWARD HUTTON, with an Introduction by
CHARLES F. RIDEAL. *[In Preparation.*

THE PAGEANT OF LIFE : An Epic or Man.
In Five Books. By GEORGE BARLOW. Second
Edition. Crown 8vo, Cloth, 6s. Post free, 4½d.
extra.

"A new poet has arisen among us ; an indisputable poet, forcible,
graceful, earnest, courageous ; having something of real interest and
great moment to say, and knowing bow to express his strong, bold
thoughts in words of extraordinary power and lines of rare beauty.
—*Daily Telegraph.*

"Of undoubted power, and quite exceptional poetical merit."—
Morning Post.

FROM DAWN TO SUNSET. By GEORGE BARLOW. Crown 8vo, Cloth, 6s. Post Free, 4½d. extra.

"In his recently published volume, 'From Dawn to Sunset,' Mr George Barlow manifests, in quite an equal degree, what he has already shown in his 'Pageant of Life,' a power sufficient to place him in the same rank with Tennyson, Swinburne, and Matthew Arnold."—*Westminster Review.*

"'From Dawn to Sunset' is an important book. As a singer Mr. Barlow can lay claim to a rank which few would question."—*Black and White.*

A LOST MOTHER. By GEORGE BARLOW.
"Dedicated to the Great Company of Mourners upon Earth, with the hope that for one and all of us comfort may be at hand." One Volume, Fcap. 4to, with Rubricated Initials, Antique Boards, 5s. A Large Paper Edition is also published at 7s. 6d. net. (Both Editions contain an excellent reproduction of one of Blake's celebrated drawings.)

"Mr. Barlow has produced a poem not only worthy of his reputation, but one likely to confirm and extend it."—*Scotsman.*

"Mr. Barlow is a sad singer; but he is amongst those who sing."—*Spectator.*

THE CRUCIFIXION OF MAN: A Narrative
Poem. By GEORGE BARLOW. With Portrait of the Author. Crown 8vo, Cloth extra, 6s. Fifty only signed Large Paper Copies, 7s. 6d. net. Post Free, 4½d. extra.

"There is much splendid versification in 'The Crucifixion of Man —*Glasgow Herald.*

"There is vigour, intellect, and great eloquence in the book. The story is powerful and interesting."—*Newcastle Chronicle.*

MEDICINE,

NURSING,

AND

ALLIED SUBJECTS

THE POPULAR MEDICAL MONTHLY, with which is incorporated THE NURSE AND CHILDHOOD. A Journal for every Household. Price One Penny. Subscription 2s. per annum. Post Free.

"Is deserving of a place in every home. '—*Blackpool Herald*.
"Welcome and cheap periodical,"—*Reading Mercury*.
"Is well worth reading,"—*Literary World*.

NURSING OLD AGE. By MARY TRUMAN, M.R.B.N.A., and EDITH SYKES, A.S.I. Paper, One Shilling ; Cloth, Half-a-crown. Post Free, 3*d*. extra.

THE PRACTICAL NURSING SERIES. By MARY TRUMAN, M.R.B.N.A., and EDITH SYKES, A.S.I.—

No. 1. "Food for the Sick." (Second Edition, Tenth Thousand.)
No. 2. "Disinfection."
No. 3. "Young Babies."
Threepence each ; Post Free, 4*d*.

"The authors are two thoroughly qualified County Council lecturers, and their recommendations are brief, easy to understand, and very practical."—*Literary World*.

ACCIDENTS By G. M. LOWE, M.D., Lecturer and Examiner to the St. John's Ambulance Association. Sixpence ; Post Free, 7*d*.

HOW TO PROLONG LIFE : An Inquiry into the Cause of "Old Age" and "Natural Death." Showing the Diet and Agents best adapted for a Lengthened Prolongation of Human Life on Earth. By C. DE LACY EVANS, M.R.C.S.E., Ph.D., Solly Medalist, St. Thomas' Hospital ; late Surgeon St. Saviour's Hospital, Surgeon Gold Coast of Africa, and Hon. Surgeon to Lady Sandhurst's Home. Third and Revised Edition. 3s. 6*d*. ; Post Free, 3*d*. extra. [*Shortly*.

THE NURSE ; or, Hygieia in Homespun. Edited by CHARLES F. RIDEAL. A Supplement to the *Popular Medical Monthly*. Price, One Penny. Subscription, 2s. per annum, Post Free.

CHILDHOOD. A Magazine for Every Mother, Edited by MARGARET E. GOOD. A Supplement to the *Popular Medical Monthly*. Price, One Penny. Subscription, 2s. per annum, post free.

OCCULT,

FOLK LORE,

ETC., ETC.

THE PALMIST AND CHIROLOGICAL RE-
VIEW, the Journal ot the Chirological Society.
Third year of issue. Edited by Mrs. KATHARINE
ST. HILL and Mr. CHARLES F. RIDEAL. Monthly
Sixpence ; post free, 6s. 6d. per annum.

„ So much interest is taken in Palmistry that many readers will be
glad to know that the Chirological Society publish a monthly journa
called the *Palmist.*"—*Dorothy's Home Journal.*

"Other contents, upon the judicious assortment and condensation
of which the editors, Mrs. Katharine St. Hill and Mr. Charles F.
Rideal, are to be congratulated,"—*Evening News and Post.*

"From the *Palmist and Chirological Review* I learn things of
interest."—*Review.*

CHIROMANCY, CHIROGNOMY, PALMISTRY.
The Art of Divining by Inspection of the Lines of
the Hand. By LANGDON TAYLOR. Eighteenpence ;
Post Free, 3d. extra. [*In Preparation.*

PRECIOUS STONES AND GEMS, WITH
THEIR REPUTED VIRTUES. Curious, Inte-
resting, and Valuable Notes. By LANGDON TAYLOR.
Eighteenpence ; Post Free, 3d. extra.
[*In Preparation*

WHOM TO MARRY. A Book all about Love
and Marriage. By MAUD WHEELER. Three Shillings and Sixpence ; Post Free, 3d. extra.
[*Shortly.*

" A concise and lucid handbook for those commencing the study
of Physiognomy."—*Bookseller.*

MOLES OR BIRTHMARKS, and their Signi-
fication to Man and Woman. By MAUD WHEELER.
Three Shillings and Sixpence ; Post Free, 3d.
extra.

" There is no lack of clearness and fulness in the instructions here
given us."—*Literary World.*

GOOD LUCK ; or, Omens and Superstitions. By
L. E. FRAPPEUR. Three Shillings and Sixpence ;
Post Free, 3d. extra. [*In Preparation.*

WORKS BY
MR. CHARLES F. RIDEAL
ISSUED THROUGH
OTHER PUBLISHERS.

STORIES FROM SCOTLAND YARD (Sixth
Thousand). By CHARLES F. RIDEAL.
Two Shillings.
George Routledge & Sons, Ltd., Ludgate Hill, E.C.

MORE PEOPLE WE MEET. By CHARLES F.
RIDEAL. Illustrated by L. RAVENHILL, MARK
ZANGWILL, etc. One Shilling.
A limited edition of signed and numbered copies at
Five Shillings.
Ward & Downey, Ltd., York Buildings, Adelphi, W.C.

YOUNG LADIES OF TO-DAY. By CHARLES F.
RIDEAL, with Illustrations by "CROW."
One Shilling.
A limited edition or signed and numbered copies at
Five Shillings.
Dean & Son, Ltd., 160A, Fleet Street, E.C.

THE NURSING RECORD & THE HOSPITAL
WORLD. The Representative Journal of the
Nursing Profession. Established and formerly
Edited by CHARLES F. RIDEAL. One Penny,
Weekly.
11, Adam Street, Adelphi, W.C.

THE NURSING RECORD SERIES OF
MANUALS AND TEXT BOOKS. Edited by
CHARLES F. RIDEAL.

No. 1. "Lectures to Nurses on Antiseptics in Sur-
gery." (Containing seven coloured plates.) By E.
STANMORE BISHOP, F.R.C.S. Eng.; Hon. Surgeon,
Ancoats Hospital, Manchester. Two Shillings.

No. 2. "Norris's Nursing Notes." A Manual of
Medical and Surgical Information for the use of
Hospital Nurses and others. With illustrations,
and a glossary of medical and surgical terms. By
RACHAEL NORRIS (née Williams), late Acting
Superintendent of Royal Victoria Military Hospital
at Suez, and formerly matron to St. Mary's Hos-
pital, W. Two Shillings.

No. 3. "A Manual of Practical Electro-Therapeutics."
By ARTHUR HARRIES, M.D., A.I.E.E, and H
NEWMAN LAWRENCE, M.I.E.E., with photographs
and diagrams. Eighteenpence.

No. 4. " Massage for Beginners." By LUCY FITCH.
One Shilling.
11, Adam Street, Adelphi, W.C.

THE RECORD "BOOKLET" SERIES. Edited by CHARLES F. RIDEAL,

No. 1. "Points for Probationers." By Miss E J. R. LANDALE, Member of the Royal British Nurses' Association. One Shilling.

No. 2. "Fever Nursing." A Course of Lectures on the Nursing required in cases of Ordinary Fever. By Miss MARY HARRIS, Matron of the Suffolk General Hospital, Bury St. Edmunds; formerly Matron of the Fever Hospital, Carlisle, and Sister at the Borough Fever Hospital, Leeds.
One Shilling.
11, Adam Street, Adelphi, W.C.

A DIGEST OF LITERATURE. The Student's Series of Handbooks. By CHARLES F. RIDEAL and LIONEL M. HAWKINS.

No. 1. **English Prose.**
No. 2. **English Poetry.**
No. 3. **The English Drama.**
Jarrold and Sons, Paternoster Row, E.C.

[*In Preparation*

www.ingramcontent.com/pod-product-compliance
Lightning Source LLC
Chambersburg PA
CBHW030602270326
41927CB00007B/1009